香港國際詩歌之夜 *2013*
INTERNATIONAL POETRY NIGHTS IN HONG KONG

編輯 Editors

北島 Bei Dao

陳嘉恩 Shelby K. Y. Chan

方梓勳 Gilbert C. F. Fong

柯夏智 Lucas Klein

馬德松 Christopher Mattison

彼得·明特
Peter Minter

目錄 Contents

1 Never Return to a Meadow Permit

You began as it ends to begin, holy world
calling up a wind as you walk out

& stand before the crest
to speak of love, living in the shape of people,
breath's slow fall

with no memory of form, like
all that is made of grass, stone, sleep in trees

grows taller and taller with extinction.
Tonight's town
drinks up an army of ghosts,

screens tinkle as new ice
explodes gracefully overhead, blue deals transmitted
to fields of occupation.

You are there in a dream
opening on the hour, light fall of leaves
commodity's source

in each word, line, leaf
as it passes daily from our lives.

I am permitted to never return
to a meadow, the one they show again on cable
eyes breezy with rites

of chaos, that permission,
now propertied & lost, is gone.

永不重返一片草地許可

在它結束以便開始之時，你開始，神聖的世界
召集一陣風，你走了出去

並在山頂面前站定
談及愛，居於人民的形狀中，
呼吸緩慢的墜落

已忘卻形式，猶如
草、石頭和樹中睡眠組成的一切

越來越高，越來越高，伴隨著熄滅。
今夜的鎮子
飲盡一支幽靈大軍，

螢幕叮噹作響，彷彿新冰
優雅地在頭頂爆炸，藍色的冷杉傳播
直至被佔的田野。

你在那裏，在一個
正點開門的夢裏，葉子輕盈的飄落
日用品的源頭

在每個詞語，句子，葉片裏
當它每日從我們的生活經過時。

我得到許可，永不重返
一片草地，那片他們在電視上再次展示的草地
眼睛因為混亂的禮儀

而愉悦，那份許可，
如今擁有而又喪失，已經逝去。

（高興譯）

2 The Roadside Bramble

Walking late by a roadside bramble
Hoops of brittle thorn, a caul of dead grass, quiet rust
Frost-burnt une feuille serrate
Motes fall and swirl as brassy notes and cobwebs
Tangle straw stems in mossy dirt, the gravel wash
A stripped page of newspaper rotting, crushed
Polyethylene terephthalate
Half-full of piss or rain water, the sign of a dog
Chalk eroded in the furrow of a wheel
Gone a little wide on the corner, or a near miss
Now overgrown in parochial paspalum, afternoon light
Cold and real, bees somewhere in the shadows
A thought of honey in the thicket
The grey common behind a wire fence half down in the
    damp
Bruise hung on the smoke
Of a sundog burnt in hazy sky, translucent
Sleep stuck in the cavernous dawn of a bramble there
    by the roadside
Where I hurry into the emaciated past
Where dry straw recedes speechless into the middle

distance
A skein of mist settling over a paddock
Air still, damp, muddy in my nose as the scent of blood
Steel cold hockey bone blue, knee high
Twigs and the hair on my skin lift in the golden
    aperture
Of the sky's milk crystal
Fanned behind a brittle stand of eight grey poplars
Pines melting in the middle distance
Dark green glass shards sliding into the earth
A path trodden flakes of rock
Through clumps and bristles of grass and wet-stemmed
    seed-heads
Drooping over bright plastic bits and rusting caps
Squashed with dirt into a bleak loam
A field scattered with the bones of my predecessors
Wandering aimlessly over turquoise hills, smoky dead
    trees
I find I'm outside the future, overgrown
Great walls of roots & earth crumbling sodden in the
    muddy weather

Wooden claws of hackberry gum
Knotted foetal in the grey wind, contrail chords in the
    sky
Lines unfurling between hard matter and blue
Blown above a jetliner's silver precipice
Disappearing into the end of a broken branch
Time and space are orange as mud in gravel
Trees a-glint with a wild fire
Sparks flying across the horizon the singular grey abyss
Every bramble has been the same, I think
As they all rush from my past like black swans, snow
    geese
Drawn into the circle of gravel
A formation of birds dropping suddenly into mind
As I walk around, feathers widening
Angular as they land into the poverty of the world
The horizon always looming, then retreating from the
    present
And all it holds, the skeletal frame of a sparrow chick
Its absent eye resting on a quartz pebble
Left as a sign to the logic of inhuman death, clear,

immensely old
A grain of cold stone, the indifferent raw tangle
In a bracken fern halo, the silent forehead of a sickle
    moon
Tacked strangely to a wooden light-pole
The sound of water tinkling and gurgling, treble & bass
A silver banner fluttering and wending
Through the poplars and brace of pines
Darkness somehow equal to its bright and random
    melody
Caught in the cold pomegranate at the road's end
Crimson flesh held in a world of white foam
Mist correlates, transpires, solid shapes beneath the
    moon
& stars, hips and haws, love and hate
No matter how opaque and powerless I become
I still cry into the night as it springs burning into
    felony
Emptiness glowing through dry yellow stalks
No match for the whorl at the crown of your head
Telescoped to a galaxy, a whale from the old world bare

As a chunky key-ring nob lost in the mossy grit
Where I walk & look, no doubt within
Perhaps hell-bent as gravel paths spread from me
   chaotically
All the same, having wandered here before
And knowing how each will always yield its own
I fall away into the roadside ditch
Sticks and mud stuck in my hair, the back of my throat
Catching the gold sunset
Behind, of course, bitumen spread Bauhaus thin and
   black
A wall of glass windows over the road
A mercury pool shimmering in the wind
The whole reflected world shuddering.

路邊黑刺莓

遲暮漫步，走過路邊黑刺莓
尖利的刺環，一團枯死的草，靜靜的鏽跡
Frost-burnt une feuille serrate
塵埃飄落，旋動，一如刺耳的音符，蜘蛛網
糾纏著草梗，在佈滿苔蘚的塵土裏，沙礫清洗
一頁剝落的報紙腐爛，碾碎
聚乙烯對苯二甲酸酯
半是尿或雨水，狗的跡象
白堊腐蝕，在角落的車轍中
擴展了些許，或者幾近失蹤
此刻在堂區雀椑蔓延，午後的光
清冷，真切，蜜蜂在陰影中某處
念及灌木叢中的蜂蜜
灰色的公用草地，在潮濕中一半倒塌的鐵絲網後面
青腫懸掛在燃燒的
日狗的煙霧中，在朦朧的天空中，半透明
睡眠沉入一棵黑刺莓洞穴般的黃昏，就在路邊
那裏，我匆匆走進衰弱的往昔
那裏，乾草默默退往中間距離
一縷霧靄停駐在一座圍場的上空
空氣凝滯，潮濕，泥濘，在我的鼻子裏，猶如血的

味道

冰冷的鋼冰球骨架，高高的膝蓋

細枝，和我皮膚上的毛髮在天空

那牛奶水晶金色的縫隙裏

一排冷漠的灰色楊樹，總共八棵，後面

松柏融化在中間距離

深綠色玻璃碎片滑進土地

一條小徑踩著岩石塊穿過

叢叢縷縷的草木，莖稈潮濕的種子穗

低垂於亮麗的塑膠嚼子和鏽跡斑斑的便帽上

夾雜著塵土，擠進荒涼的壤土

一片田野散佈著我祖輩的遺骨

漫無目的地徜徉，在綠松石山丘的上方，在死寂的

　　煙霧濛濛的林子的上方

我發現我身處未來之外，蔓延

巨大的根泥牆，濕漉漉的，在泥濘的氣候中瓦解

樸樹膠木爪

胎兒般糾結於灰色的風中，煙弦在天際

線舒展，在硬物質和蔚藍之間

一架噴氣式班機的銀懸崖被吹到天上

消隱於一棵斷枝的盡頭

時空橙黃，一如沙礫中的泥沼
樹林微微閃爍，帶著一團野性的火
火花飛過地平線，那孤獨的灰色深淵
每株黑刺莓都別無二致，我想
它們全都黑天鵝般從我的過去沖出，雪雁
被引入沙礫圓圈
一隊鳥兒突然闖進腦海
當我四處漫遊時，羽翼拓寬
骨瘦如豺，當它們降落在世界的貧瘠中
地平線總是隱約出現，然後從現時和其
掌控的一切撤離，一隻雛雀的骨骼
它那缺席的眼停留於一顆石英卵石
作為非人類死亡邏輯的符號存留，清晰，無比古老
一粒冷石，那無動於衷的粗鄙的糾纏
在一道蕨的光暈中，鐮月寂靜的額頭
怪異地縫在一個木光極上
水聲叮叮噹當，咕咕作響，高音和低音
一面銀色的旗幟在飄揚，前行
穿過楊樹和一對松樹
黑暗不知怎的總是等於它那明媚而有即興的樂曲
在路的盡頭那棵寒冷的石榴樹上被人逮住

深紅的肉體包含在一個白色泡沫的世界裏
霧靄並置，散發，月亮和星星下面堅固的
輪廓，薔薇果和山楂果，愛與恨
不管我變得多麼晦暗和無力
我依然會哭喊著融入黑夜，當它躍動著燃成大火時
空無閃爍，穿越乾燥的黃梗
無法與你頭冠上的螺紋匹配
嵌入銀河，一條赤露的鯨魚，來自古老的世界
像枚粗壯的鑰匙圈，遺失在佈滿苔蘚的沙粒中
我在那裏漫步，觀望，毫無疑問
興許義無反顧，猶如沙路從我內心紊亂地伸展
全都一樣，曾經在此徜徉
明白每種植物總會結出自己的果實
我掉進路邊溝壕
枝條和淤泥黏進我的頭髮，我的喉嚨後面
捉住那金色的日落
背後，當然，瀝青鋪展包豪斯，單薄，黝黑
路上一堵玻璃窗牆
一座水銀池在風中閃爍
全部反射出顫抖的世界。

（高興譯）

3 The Clearing

high on abstraction
& a

distance
of mountains we form a colony   the air is
    clean the water

rainwater
we have music & books & peace   on a radio we
    listen to
the world
death itself & death itself & the cities be killed &
    ruined.

—Michael Dransfield, *The Change*

Surreal night   fog pixelates eyes   god
It is so transparent in the blue   *open them*   make
    time a queen
Drove the fire still going, stoked   flares again while
    I make coffee
A tiger in the green pine, sunrise fur   where does

the pine-cone go?

You ask   I look again   almost a breath at the
window

How can I leave the moment you arrive   asking for
milk?

Japanese maples sprout like grass   we dig the future

Branches over the spring-water creek, wet brown leaf
mulch

Red rain boots   velvet leaves drop propaganda over
the flat island

Of violets   an abandoned colony of camellia flowers

Collapses as we pass   pure white perfumed flakes
fall into pools

Of bracken water   a garden hose wound-up green
in a bin of water

A concrete Diana decays   half-life classical

Next morning winter spills into us   sudden cold

Inside, a paper cut   I taste your blood for the first
time   maroon rust

In brittle leaves   cold red stain in the dark grey sky

Keen iron we flow forever down the road   grass

boats

Sent down the sun   you are the same as us   here
    we are

Look through glass at a sea of yellow   it happens in
    time

As great distant lights approach one another

Like snow flakes to melt at the same place   the
    clearing

I am already a hole in the world   you stop me

From walking   *look at our shadows!*   my
    silhouette burns

A black hole right through the earth   one day I will
    fall

Perfectly into it, leading the way for you   (I am
    sorry

with life I have also brought you death, a halo of
    darkness

We wave to the new darkness as if it is nothing   &

The world condenses   as reverie   perhaps you
    will remember

We once stood together over the road   blocked the

sun

Laughed   a yellow daisy in your left hand
    making a world
To make a self   the self is not the world   no
We move through the late lake of day like gold koi
    light falls
Shafts of amber coil into memory   a soft crimson
    fern   unfurls

林中空地

高高的，在抽象概念和山的

距離上，我們組成一個殖民地　　空氣清新
水

雨水
我們擁有音樂和書籍和寧靜　　在收音機上
傾聽世界
讓死亡本身和死亡本身和城市被殺戮
和毀滅
　　——邁克爾·德朗斯費爾德，《變化》

超現實的夜晚　　霧模糊眼睛　　上帝
藍色中，如此的透明　　*打開*它們
將　　時間封為女王
推動依然在行走的火，撥旺　　再次燃燒
在我在沏咖啡時
一隻虎在綠松木裏，火紅的皮毛　　松果
去到哪裏？
你問　　我再次觀望　　幾近窗口的一縷呼吸
我怎能離去在你來　　要牛奶時？

雞爪楓草一般抽芽　　我們挖掘未來
樹枝俯身在泉水灣上，潮濕、金黃的樹葉覆蓋層
紅雨靴　　天鵝絨葉子在平坦的
紫羅蘭島上
撒下宣傳　　一塊被遺棄的山茶花殖民地
坍塌，在我們經過時　　純粹、白色、芬芳的葉片
飄入歐洲蕨水
池塘　　一根捲起的綠色的花園澆水管
在一箱水裏
一個清晰的狄安娜在衰敗　　古典的半衰期
翌晨，冬日灑進我們　　突然，寒冷
裏面，一張剪紙　　我頭一回嚐
你的血　　紫紅色鐵鏽
在易碎的葉子裏　　寒冷的紅污點在深灰的天空中
鋒利的鐵我們總在路上流動　　草船
太陽降落　　你同我們一樣
我們來到這裏
透過玻璃望著一片黃色的海　　它
及時發生
猶如遠處的光互相貼近
就像雪片在相同的地點融化　　林中空地

我已是世上的一個洞　　　你讓我
停住步子　　瞧瞧我們的影子！　　　我的
剪影在燃燒
一個黑洞穿越地球　　有一天，我將完美地
掉進洞裏，為你引路　　　（真是抱歉
我為你帶來生，也帶來死，一圈黑暗
我們朝嶄新的黑暗揮手，彷彿它是空無
世界凝凍　　猶如幻想　　　興許你將記得
我們曾一道站在路上　　　堵住太陽
大笑　　你的左手握著一支黃雛菊花
製造一個世界
為了製造一個自我　　自我並非世界　　　不
我們金錦鯉般移過遲到的白晝之湖
光線降臨
琥珀箭簇繞進記憶　　一棵柔軟、深紅的
蕨　　　展開

（高興譯）

4 In the Serious Light of Nothing

Light dries out on the white kitchen
Window frame, cold plain and dust, the hard world

Fiery on the east side, late on the west.
High on the high wall the shadow of a lion

Fur fur of a lion hung on a wall, a passing shadow.
I pick up a glass and look at the light

There are eucalypts and kookaburras and lyre birds
Fuck me, a series of days reaching into the desert

Every day darker through my old orange filter
A swampy river shimmering with laughter.

Out in the real I shiver in a bright way.
Pink camellia flowers fount over the 1940s

House-brick porch, last century collapsing into the
    present
As if each year were a flower all of a sudden

Catching the rays as they fall interminably forward
Over the roofline and into the garden,

Your chiffon number caught in the lavender
Glistening dew on the sticky wet seed row.

Tell me, were they in love back then, really like
They said they were, and are we

Felt like pollen through the rays, your hand on its
    descent
Leaving whirlpools of darkness in the air?

Easy bees navigate around, sip water from miniature
    beaches
Along the spring-feed creek,

Not a cloud in the sky, just white cockatoos
Spilt from snow gum limbs and sun flaring off the
    ridge.

I watch the breeze in the hair on your forearm,
A word on your lips about to take flight.

在嚴肅的虛無之光中

光枯竭，在白色的廚房
窗框上，寒冷的平原和塵土，那艱難的世界

東面激烈無比，東面天色已晚。
高高的在高牆上，一隻獅子皮毛的影子，一隻

獅子的皮毛掛在一堵牆上，一個流逝的影子。
我撿起一片眼鏡，細看那光

有桉葉油，有笑翠鳥，有琴鳥
他媽的，一連串的日子進入沙漠

日益幽暗，經過我那古老的橙黃色篩檢程式
一條沼澤般的河流在笑聲中閃爍。

外面，在現實中，我以歡快的方式顫慄。
粉紅的山茶花，一九四零年代磚牆門廊

上面的源泉，上個世紀掉進現時
彷彿每年都是一朵花，突然

抓住光線，在它們無休無止地墜向
屋頂輪廓線上和花園裏，

你的雪紡綢號碼在薰衣草裏被捉住
閃爍的露珠，在一排粘稠潮濕的種子裏。

告訴我，那時，真如他們所説，他們在
戀愛嗎？我們真如花粉穿越那道道光線，

當你將手放在它的下降上，
在空中離開黑暗的漩渦的時刻？

安逸的蜜蜂四處飛行，沿著春潤河
從微型海灘啜飲水，

天上沒有一絲雲，唯有白鳳頭鸚鵡
從金合歡葉片中跌落，太陽閃耀著滑下山脊。

我望著你前臂毛髮裏的微風，
一個詞語在你的唇上，即將飛翔。

（高興譯）

5 Cleaning Flakes from Grass

Declaring past
          concrete & masonry
ridge bound, light perceived first green
tessellated banksia
          brushed forward against blue wind
          & chipped

Evening morning passes
          grass's contamination
white lead
flakes slow curl around stone, blades
          debris & coincidental
          cell drifting

Lines I improve, boundaries erode
          discontinuous nature
& the Sun's Modern Glare, just as
pigment ratio can supply
          chlorophyll for Malevich's
          Taking in the Rye

Or gloss correa's flower
       & vibration as pollen, war's vanguard
brief to crest an edge
of blank elements of reference, the bright
       Pacific's serious technologies
       timing spray below

Each flake, or strip of paint
       picked by the eye & equal as
a handful to centuries of earth, mock
canvas split blue by fine
       contrails radiating north
       Overhead to America.

清除草上的雪片

宣告著經過
　　混泥土和磚石建築
山脊纏繞，光首先感覺到綠色的
飾有棋盤花紋的山龍眼
　　頂著藍色的風擠向前去
　　被切成碎片

夜晚早晨穿越
　　草的感染
白色的鉛
雪片緩緩在石頭周圍捲曲，葉子
　　殘骸和純屬巧合的
　　細胞漂流

我改善的線條，邊界腐蝕
　　不連貫的自然
和太陽的現代強光，就像
顏料比率能為馬列維奇的
　　《耕種黑麥》
　　提供葉綠素

或者給科雷亞花塗上光澤
　　震顫一如花粉，戰爭先鋒
對峰頂扼要表明
全部參照要素的邊緣，那明媚的
　　太平洋嚴肅的技藝
　　每只薄片下面的

定時噴灑，或者一抹油彩
　　被眼睛撿起，等同於
幾個世紀的地球，嘲弄
畫布分裂的藍，經由細膩的
　　凝跡，在北方上空
　　發光，朝向美洲。

（高興譯）

6 Valentinea

I desire craft so short to learn,
every bough made gold & black
so green it is just figurative
floating exactly unillumined in the purchase
shade affords, the house over there
entering late summer, modernity's heaven
as birds strafe the air with skilful council
accumulated easy during dusk.
You will stand here forever, indelible
feet marking river banks in salty negatives
empty and fulfilled for their solicitude,
small creatures' disorderly expanse
in prints offered like romance to erosion,
decay, originals of revisable originals
year by year bent calligraphically in place.
Darkened copies are selectively embraced,
entangled as they sometimes vaguely are
with fair realism, fountains over rocks.
I am Cupid with a kite, light & legless
on a route apprehended only in the soft sun
naturally as worms or goats *of which*

I tell no tale, their quiet feeding & donation
peeling from this silence, like a life.

瓦倫廷納

我渴望如此快速學會的手藝，
每棵樹枝都讓金子和黑色
綠得成為比喻，未經啟發，
飄浮在陰影所承擔得起的
購置中，那邊的那幢房子
進入晚夏，現代性的天堂
猶如鳥兒，在黃昏輕易積聚，
用充滿技巧的會議轟炸天空
你將永遠站立於此，堅持的
足，出於擔心，在尖銳的否定中
標示河岸，空曠而又滿足，
渺小生物混亂無序的膨脹
在印製品中恰似即將腐蝕的羅曼司，
衰敗，修訂版原作中的原作，
年復一年，字體彎曲在適當的位置。
變黑的複件得到選擇性的接納，
纏繞，正如它們有時隱約包含
美好的現實，山岩上的噴泉。
我是帶風箏的丘比特，輕盈，無腿，
所走線路僅在柔和的光中被人領會，
同蠕蟲和山羊一般自然，*關於它們*

我無故事可講，它們靜靜的餵養，
和這沉寂中脫落的捐贈，宛若生命。

（高興譯）

彼得・明特是澳洲重要詩人、編輯和詩學作家。1967年出生，兼有蘇格蘭、英格蘭和澳洲土著三種血統。他先在海邊後又在叢林裡長大，18歲時旅行前往日本，隨後在悉尼大學攻讀文學和哲學。著有多部詩集，其中包括《空蕩蕩的德克薩斯》、《早晨》、《連字型大小》以及《藍草》。他的作品發表於眾多澳洲和國際刊物和選集，並曾為他贏得無數獎學金、資助和獎項。自從1990年代起，他一直是澳洲先鋒詩歌和詩學的核心人物。他組織過不少詩歌活動，以及視覺藝術、音樂和詩歌展覽，還編輯或參與編輯《伐樓拿》、《柯達炸藥》、《花萼：澳洲當代詩人三十家》等多種詩歌冊子、詩歌選本和詩歌雜誌。近期，還參與編輯了《安琪拉吉》雜誌「生態詩學和教育學」專號。目前，他是澳洲最主要的文學和思想雜誌《轉地放牧》編輯。作為詩人、理論家和教師，明特在作品中重新思考了澳洲和新西蘭詩歌語言、物質主義地緣哲學，以及自然和詩歌生態學之間的關係。他的近期作品對土著「家鄉」概念以及澳洲想像去殖民化主題進行了生態詩學探索。他在悉尼大學擔任高級講師，主要研究澳洲和土著詩歌、詩學和生態詩學。他與詩人、音樂家和學者凱特・法甘以及他們的兩個孩子居住在藍山。

Peter Minter is a leading Australian poet, editor and writer on poetics. Born in 1967, he shares Scottish, English and Aboriginal heritage. He grew up first by the ocean and then in the bush, traveled to Japan at the age of eighteen and then studied literature and philosophy at the University of Sydney. He is the author of several books of poetry, including *Empty Texas*, *Morning*, *Hyphen* and *blue grass*. His work has been published widely and anthologized regularly in Australia and internationally, and he has been awarded numerous fellowships, grants and prizes. Since the mid-1990s he has been a central figure in innovative and avant-garde Australian poetry and poetics. Apart from curating various renowned poetry events and exhibitions of visual art, music and poetry, he was the founding editor of the *Varuna New Poetry* broadsheets, the founding co-editor of *Cordite*, a co-editor of the influential anthology *Calyx: 30 Contemporary Australian Poets*, the poetry editor of the leading Australian journal *Meanjin*, and a co-editor of both the groundbreaking *Macquarie PEN Anthology of Aboriginal Literature* and *The Literature of Australia*. He recently co-edited the "Ecopoetics and Pedagogies" special issue of *Angelaki: Journal of the Theoretical Humanities*, and is now poetry editor of Australia's foremost radical journal of literature and ideas, *Overland*. As a poet, theorist and teacher, Minter reconsiders in his works antipodean encounters between poetic language, materialist geophilosophies and the rendering of natural and poetic ecologies. His recent work has focused especially on an ecopoetical inquiry into Aboriginal conceptions of "Country" and the decolonization of the Australian imagination. He is a senior lecturer in English at the University of Sydney, specializing in Australian and Aboriginal poetry, poetics and ecopoetics, and lives in the Blue Mountains with poet, musician and scholar Kate Fagan, and their two children.

出版 Publisher
香港中文大學出版社 The Chinese University Press

封面影像 Cover Image
北島 Bei Dao

出版日期 Date of Publication
二零一三年十一月 November 2013

國際書號 ISBN
978-962-996-619-5

香港國際詩歌之夜 2013 International Poetry Nights in Hong Kong 2013
主辦單位 Organizers
香港中文大學文學院 Faculty of Arts, The Chinese University of Hong Kong
香港浸會大學文學院 Faculty of Arts, Hong Kong Baptist University
香港科技大學人文社會科學學院 School of Humanities and Social Science,
The Hong Kong University of Science and Technology

合作夥伴 In Partnership With
英國文化協會 British Council

協辦單位 Co-organizers
時刻文化 Moment Communications
香港中文大學出版社 The Chinese University Press

贊助 Sponsors
香港兆基創意書院 HKICC Lee Shau Kee School of Creativity
中國會 The China Club
周凱旋基金會 Chau Hoi Shuen Foundation

Printed in Hong Kong